# THE STUARTS

A ROYAL HISTORY OF ENGLAND

# THE STUARTS

BY MAURICE ASHLEY

EDITED BY
ANTONIA FRASER

University of California Press
Berkeley   Los Angeles

University of California Press
Berkeley and Los Angeles, California

Published by arrangement with Cassell & Co

The text of *The Stuarts* is taken from the single-volume
*The Lives of the Kings & Queens of England*, first published in the United Kingdom
in 1975 by Weidenfeld & Nicolson, revised in 1993 and 1998.

Text copyright © Cassell & Co 2000
Design and layout copyright © Cassell & Co 2000

Cataloging-in-Publication data is on file with the Library of Congress.

ISBN 0-520-228000-6 *2824 6956 12/02*

Jacket images: front © Weidenfeld & Nicolson Archives (imaginary scene of James 1 and his
family listening to a sermon at St Paul's cross by John Gipkyn); back © The Bridgeman Art
Library, London (Charles 1 on horseback, with Monsieur Saint Antoine, by Sir Anthony van Dyck).

*Endpapers*: 'Ladies and Cavaliers in a Ballroom' by Abraham Bosse. *Page 2*: 'William and Mary
Enthroned' by Sir John Thornhill.

Printed and bound in Italy.
9  8  7  6  5  4  3  2  1

# CONTENTS

# INTRODUCTION

When Elizabeth died in 1603, the question of her succession reached its climax. Elizabeth never named an heir and her crown went to James VI of Scotland, son of Mary Stuart, Queen of Scots. In his person, James united the two crowns of Scotland and England and, by becoming James I of England, he also became the first monarch of Great Britain.

Despite his desire for a proper union of these two nations and his genuine love of peace, James I has received a censorious press and has been unfairly crushed between the success of Queen Elizabeth I and the English Civil War. He has also incited strong moral disapproval, mostly predicated on the events of his private life. But James I should in fact be remembered as a successful and learned man who was worthy of his position as the first king of Great Britain, who presided over a flourishing literary age and who was intimately connected with that jewel of our literature, the Authorised Version of the Bible.

It was James' second son, Charles, who succeeded in 1625. Charles I, 'The Royal Martyr', can fairly claim to be the most ill-used of monarchs. Defeated by his subjects in battle, he endured the extreme fate of death at their hands after the pretence of a legal trial. His family fled to France and the Crown remained in abeyance for the next eleven years.

But this most unfortunate king was at the same time England's most crucial ruler, and the two opposing views of him need reconciling: was Charles the helpless puppet of uncontainable social forces, or was he a narrow-minded bigot who, through his own thoughtless aboslutism, provoked the Civil War? The peculiar character of Charles I is central to the complicated politics and social tensions of the time.

Following Charles I's death on the scaffold in 1649, his eldest surviving son, Charles, was intent upon securing the kingship of England and Scotland. He was crowned King of the Scots in 1651, but it was not until 1660 and the death of Oliver Cromwell that he regained the throne of England. Charles II was unanimously welcomed back by the triumphant Royalists. It was a critical moment for the monarchy and Charles II had to rule over a country divided by civil war and a republican regime.

He nonetheless succeeded in reconciling the old Church of England and the Presbyterians and, in contrast to the turbulence both before and after his reign, a sort of peace prevailed (so much so that we think back to 'good King Charles' and his golden reign). But the period of Restoration is also best known for its court luxuries and frivolities, lax moral standards, comedy theatre and royal mistresses, from Nell Gwynne, the saucy actress, to Louise de Kéroualle.

Charles II died in 1685 and his failure to provide a legitimate heir condemned the country to the care of his unsatisfactory brother, James II. As a young man, James was one of the most attractive and affable of the exiled Royal entourage. In 1648 he made a sensational getaway from the grasp of Parliament dressed as a woman. But, twenty years later, his conversion to Catholicism and subsequent unstinted allegiance towards the proselytisation of the Catholic faith, proved critical for England and the monarchy. The country James II ruled was by now resolutely Protestant. In the throes of fighting off William of Orange, the husband of his Protestant daughter, Mary, James fled, and the once dashing young duke spent the rest of his years in melancholy, albeit pious, exile in France.

The political marriage and joint rule of William and Mary ushered in a new era and a new constitution for England. A series of Acts limited the power of the monarchy in favour of Parliament and an entirely new concept of kingship was born from the 'Glorious Revolution': the concept of constitutional monarchy.

Mary's sister, Anne, is the last of the Stuart sovereigns and her life is something of a Cinderella story. On the death of her brother-in-law, William, in 1702, Anne found herself the only contender to the throne. Upright, conscientious, essentially English, yet shy and gout-ridden, Anne was appointed to represent the once powerful and fascinating House of Stuart.

For twelve years she presided over an age of unequalled triumphs in the sphere of war, and unequalled intrigues in the sphere of politics. But Queen Anne's inability to produce a surviving child despite seventeen pregnancies meant that the Whigs and the Tories had to balance the possible succession of her Jacobite brother against that of the Protestant Hanoverians.

# THE STUARTS

## 1603-1714

JAMES I 1603-25
CHARLES I 1625-49
CHARLES II 1660-85
JAMES II 1685-8
WILLIAM III 1688-1702 and MARY II 1688-94
ANNE 1702-14

*Opposite:* King Charles I on horseback, with Monsieur Saint Antoine, by
Sir Anthony van Dyck (1599–1641). Charles I was a connoisseur as well as
a shrewd observer of the power of the arts to increase the dignity and
stature of rulers: he and Van Dyck made a speciality of equestrian portraits
modelled on those of antiquity and the Renaissance.

# THE TUDORS AND STUARTS

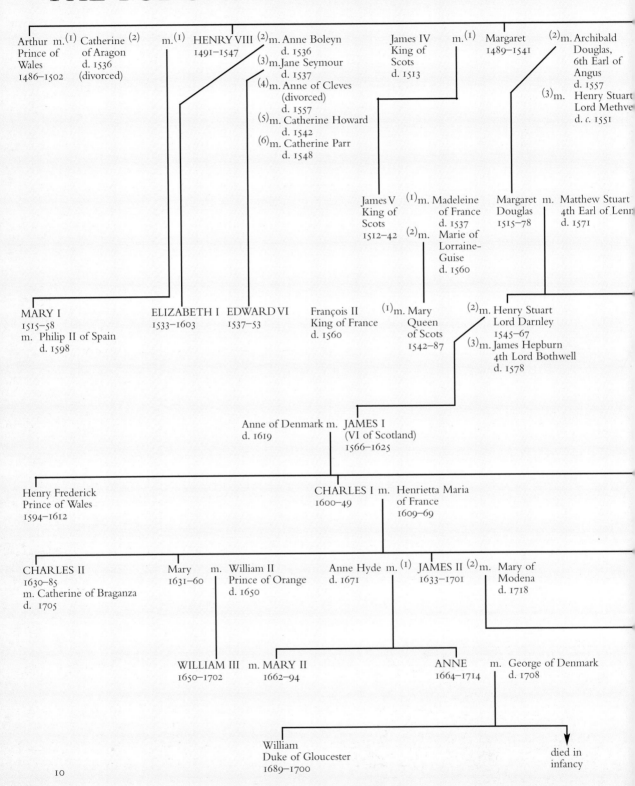

Arthur m.(1) Catherine (2) m.(1) HENRY VIII (2)m. Anne Boleyn
Prince of of Aragon 1491–1547 d. 1536
Wales d. 1536 (3)m.Jane Seymour
1486–1502 (divorced) d. 1537
(4)m. Anne of Cleves
(divorced)
d. 1557
(5)m. Catherine Howard
d. 1542
(6)m. Catherine Parr
d. 1548

James IV m.(1) Margaret (2)m. Archibald
King of 1489–1541 Douglas,
Scots 6th Earl of
d. 1513 Angus
d. 1557
(3)m. Henry Stuart
Lord Methve
d. c. 1551

James V (1)m. Madeleine Margaret m. Matthew Stuart
King of of France Douglas 4th Earl of Lenn
Scots d. 1537 1515–78 d. 1571
1512–42 (2)m. Marie of
Lorraine-
Guise
d. 1560

MARY I
1515–58
m. Philip II of Spain
d. 1598

ELIZABETH I EDWARD VI
1533–1603 1537–53

François II (1)m. Mary (2)m. Henry Stuart
King of France Queen Lord Darnley
d. 1560 of Scots 1545–67
1542–87 (3)m. James Hepburn
4th Lord Bothwell
d. 1578

Anne of Denmark m. JAMES I
d. 1619 (VI of Scotland)
1566–1625

Henry Frederick CHARLES I m. Henrietta Maria
Prince of Wales 1600–49 of France
1594–1612 1609–69

CHARLES II Mary m. William II Anne Hyde m.(1) JAMES II (2)m. Mary of
1630–85 1631–60 Prince of Orange d. 1671 1633–1701 Modena
m. Catherine of Braganza d. 1650 d. 1718
d. 1705

WILLIAM III m. MARY II ANNE m. George of Denmark
1650–1702 1662–94 1664–1714 d. 1708

William
Duke of Gloucester
1689–1700

died in
infancy

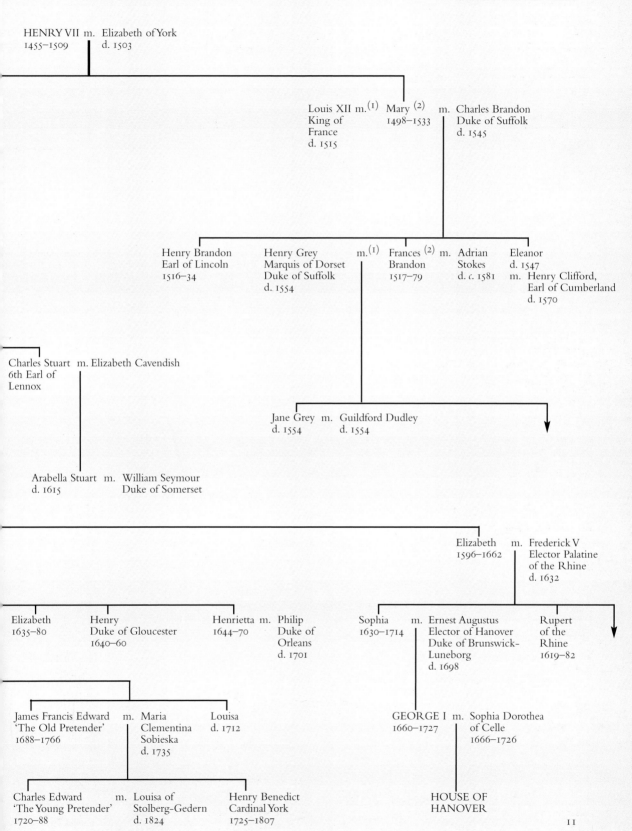

HENRY VII m. Elizabeth of York
1455–1509    d. 1503

Louis XII m.(1) Mary (2) m. Charles Brandon
King of       1498–1533    Duke of Suffolk
France                     d. 1545
d. 1515

Henry Brandon      Henry Grey        m.(1) Frances (2) m. Adrian    Eleanor
Earl of Lincoln    Marquis of Dorset        Brandon         Stokes     d. 1547
1516–34            Duke of Suffolk          1517–79         d. c. 1581  m. Henry Clifford,
                   d. 1554                                              Earl of Cumberland
                                                                       d. 1570

Charles Stuart  m. Elizabeth Cavendish
6th Earl of
Lennox

Jane Grey  m.  Guildford Dudley
d. 1554        d. 1554

Arabella Stuart  m.  William Seymour
d. 1615              Duke of Somerset

Elizabeth  m.  Frederick V
1596–1662      Elector Palatine
               of the Rhine
               d. 1632

Elizabeth     Henry              Henrietta m. Philip      Sophia      m.  Ernest Augustus       Rupert
1635–80       Duke of Gloucester 1644–70      Duke of     1630–1714       Elector of Hanover    of the
              1640–60                         Orleans                     Duke of Brunswick-    Rhine
                                              d. 1701                     Luneborg              1619–82
                                                                         d. 1698

James Francis Edward  m.  Maria        Louisa          GEORGE I  m. Sophia Dorothea
'The Old Pretender'       Clementina   d. 1712         1660–1727    of Celle
1688–1766                 Sobieska                                  1666–1726
                          d. 1735

Charles Edward      m.  Louisa of          Henry Benedict       HOUSE OF
'The Young Pretender'   Stolberg-Gedern    Cardinal York        HANOVER
1720–88                 d. 1824            1725–1807

11

# THE ARMS OF
# THE STUARTS

WHEN JAMES VI OF SCOTLAND INHERITED the English throne a change in the royal arms was necessary in order to include James's other kingdom. The resultant arms are here illustrated. The shield has been divided into four grand quarters. The old French and English quartered arms, as used for about two hundred years, were put in the first and fourth quarters. The Scottish lion within its *double tressure flory counterflory* was assigned the second quarter, whilst the harp of Ireland made its début in the royal coat in the third quarter.

Although Ireland had been raised from a lordship to a kingdom by Henry VIII and although the badge of a harp had been associated with Ireland, no proper arms of dominion existed. This was put right in the new version of the royal arms.

The supporters of the Scottish royal arms were two unicorns and so the Tudor dragon supporter was replaced by one of the Scottish unicorns. As King of Scotland, James and his successors used the arms in a different manner. The Scottish lion changed places with the English and French coats; the Scottish crest and motto replaced the English and the supporters changed sides and were depicted in a slightly different manner.

When William III and Mary II became joint sovereigns William as Prince of Orange could have added a complex quartered coat but opted for a little shield (illustrated below the arms of the Stuarts) of the arms of Nassau, which he placed in the centre of the Stuart coat. These arms are today the royal arms of Holland.

After William's death without issue the Crown passed to Mary's sister Anne but, as she did not succeed her brother-in-law as a hereditary Statholder in the Netherlands, she dropped the arms of Nassau and reverted to the Stuart royal arms until, in 1707, the two kingdoms of England and Scotland were united to form 'one Kingdom by the Name of Great Britain'. As the Act for the Union with Scotland provided that the arms of the United Kingdom shall be 'as Her Majesty shall appoint', they were duly altered.

# THE ROYAL ARMS
## 1707-1837

THE ALTERATION MADE IN THE ROYAL ARMS to reflect the union of England and Scotland was as illustrated. The arms of the two countries were placed side by side in the first and last quarters, France was assigned the second quarter and Ireland stayed put. No alteration was made to crest nor supporters; these have remained unchanged from 1603 until the present day. It will be noticed that the *double tressure* which surrounds the Scottish lion is discontinued where the coat is joined to that of England. This is an old heraldic convention which affects all forms of border when arms are shown side by side, that is *impaled*.

This new version of the arms was short-lived as Anne died in 1714 and, under the terms of the Act of Settlement of 1701, George, Elector of Hanover, Duke of Brunswick and Luneburg and Arch Treasurer of the Holy Roman Empire, succeeded to the throne. Another reshuffle was called for in order to make reference to his German dominions. This was easily effected by removing the last quartering, which was only a repetition of the first, and substituting a coat divided into three, containing the two lions of Brunswick, the lion and hearts of Luneburg and the white horse of Hanover. The little shield in the centre, which will be seen in the illustration of this coat, has on it a representation of the crown of Charlemagne. This was the badge of office of the Arch Treasurer of the Empire; other members of the royal family never showed this shield.

In 1801 the royal arms were altered yet again in order to reflect better the new kingdom of Great Britain and Ireland created by the Act of Union with Ireland in 1800. The opportunity was taken to remove the French arms, an excision which some might think several hundred years overdue. The three kingdoms were each given a quartering, the arms of England being repeated in the last quarter in the cause of symmetry. The German arms were placed in the centre, thus enabling the Electoral Bonnet, which by right should have ensigned them, to be shown. This shield is illustrated whilst next to it is the same shield ensigned by the crown which replaced the bonnet in 1816. Under the terms of the Congress of Vienna the electorate, which had disappeared when Napoleon overthrew the Empire, was erected into a kingdom.

# JAMES I *r.* 1603-25

HEN ON 24 MARCH 1603 JAMES STUART ascended the English throne, he was, as he himself boasted, an experienced king. His ancestors had ruled or at any rate reigned in Scotland since the fourteenth century and James was crowned King of the Scots when he was only thirteen months old in 1567. His father, Lord Darnley, had been mysteriously murdered and his mother, Mary Queen of Scots, had first abdicated, then reclaimed the throne and finally, defeated in battle, fled to England where she was kept a prisoner in honourable captivity until her execution for treason in 1587. A regent, the fourth Earl of Morton, governed Scotland for fourteen years during James's minority.

Although James grew up in an atmosphere of civil strife he had a sound Presbyterian and classical education. When he became an adolescent, homosexual feelings were first aroused in him by a sophisticated French nobleman, D'Aubigny Lennox. In 1581 Lennox helped engineer the execution of the Regent but his power angered some of the nobility; James was kidnapped by the Earl of Gowrie and Lennox was banished. However, James was soon rescued by his supporters and in 1583, at seventeen, assumed the reins of government. When he was twenty he concluded a treaty with Queen Elizabeth I of England, a year before his mother's death. As Elizabeth was childless and his mother, who claimed to be her successor, was dead, the likelihood of James inheriting the English throne was enhanced. He devoted all his attention to remaining on friendly terms with the Queen of England, although he made formal protests about his mother's execution. In his anxiety to obtain the throne of England he even cultivated the Pope and the English Roman Catholics. In 1600 he survived a plot

*Opposite*: A formal portrait of the young James VI of Scotland attributed to Adrian Vanson, from 1595. The young king received a good and varied education and as King of England he was able to engage on a level footing with the leading philosophers and theologians of his time.

IACOBVS DEI GRATIA REX
SCOTORVM ALTATIS SVAE 8
1574

IACOBVS · 6 · D · G
SCOTORVM
ÆTA · 29 ·
1595 ·

on his life by the Gowrie family. After entering into friendly correspondence with Sir Robert Cecil his efforts were finally crowned with success. On the death of Elizabeth I, being the direct descendant of King Henry VII, James VI King of the Scots was acknowledged as the ruler of England and went happily to London.

The conditions of monarchy in England were very different from those in Scotland. There the King was little more than the first among equals. He had twice been kidnapped and held prisoner by his own subjects and though eventually he succeeded in imposing bishops upon the Kirk, the power of the General Assembly of the Scottish Church was great. In England, on the other hand, the King was the chief executive, the Supreme Governor of the Church, the possessor of hereditary wealth, the leader of his subjects in war and peace. But his authority was constitutionally limited by tradition. The English Parliament was more independent than that of Scotland. To wage war or to meet extraordinary expenses the House of Commons had to be asked to vote money for their sovereign.

Three immediate problems presented themselves to James when he reached London. The first was a growing Puritan movement which wished to sweep all Roman Catholic rites from the church services and to revert to what were claimed to be primitive usages which laid stress on preaching and prayer rather than ceremonial and sacraments. Secondly, Parliament had waxed stronger under the Tudors and the rich gentry, who provided most of the members of the Commons, were seeking to play a larger part in state as well as church affairs. Lastly, England was still at war with Spain, a war which had continued for some fifteen years. With the last problem James coped expeditiously: he concluded peace without betraying the Dutch, who were still fighting

'The Garden of Plenty': a ceremonial arch designed by Stephen Harrison for the entry of King James I into London in 1603.

*Following pages*: Painting of Nonsuch Palace during the time of James I.

*Opposite*: James I, the son of Mary Queen of Scots, had already ruled as James VI of Scotland for thirty-six years before being crowned King of England.

for their independence from the Spanish Habsburgs in Madrid. James refused even to sanction privateering, a profitable form of licensed piracy, in which the Elizabethan seafaring heroes from Drake to Raleigh had enthusiastically engaged.

With the Puritans James initially had some sympathy, for he himself had been brought up as a Calvinist. After receiving a petition from a group of representative Puritans, James summoned a conference at Hampton Court Palace between the bishops and leading Puritans, over which he presided in person. Although he was ready to offer some concessions to the Puritans, he was provoked by the suggestion that the episcopacy should be abolished and uttered the famous dictum: 'No bishop, no king.' He ordered the preparation of a new translation of the Bible which became known as the Authorised Version or King James's Bible. On the whole, his attitude to religion was fairly tolerant and eclectic. But when the famous Gunpowder Plot by Roman Catholics to blow up the Houses of Parliament on 5 November 1605 was dis-

Contemporary illustration depicting the coronation of the first Stuart King of England, James I, and his wife, Queen Anne, at Westminster 25 July 1603.

covered, James became less kind to practising Catholics; having waived the penalties against them for not attending English church services, he reimposed them.

As a result of the Gunpowder Plot James remained for some time on friendly terms with his first Parliament, which had met in March 1604; but he had an irritating way of making exaggerated claims for the rights of the monarchy. In a book which he wrote before he left Scotland called *Basilikon Doron*, printed in 1603, he stressed the patriarchal nature of kingship and compared monarchs to gods; he was fond of addressing Parliament in lofty terms extolling the supremacy of kings. Nevertheless he was a shrewd politician and actually repudiated the argument put forward by a Cambridge professor that he was above the law.

The Gunpowder Plotters, who in an act of Roman Catholic rebellion attempted to blow up the Houses of Parliament on 5 November 1605. The illustration also shows the bloody end to which they came, their heads displayed on stakes for all to see.

James VI of Scotland and I of England with Anne of Denmark. The pair married in 1589 after James had romantically braved the dangers of the Baltic and travelled to Oslo to escort his bride to be to Scotland.

*Opposite:* Anne of Denmark painted in 1617 by Paul van Somer. She married James when he was King of the Scots and bore six children, but he tired of her, preferring the company of his male favourites.

James set himself two constructive tasks: the first was to effect a complete union between the kingdoms of Scotland and England whose crowns he wore; the second was to arrange a financial deal with the House of Commons which would guarantee him a regular and permanent income. His chief minister, Sir Robert Cecil, whom James raised to be Earl of Salisbury, attempted to carry out his master's wishes. Promoted Lord Treasurer in 1608, Salisbury took advantage of a test case to levy

LA MIA GRANDEZZA DEL'ECCELSO

additional Customs – known as 'impositions' – to increase the royal revenue. Parliament would not assent to either scheme. Though James assumed the title of King of Great Britain, the Commons were not prepared to concede equal rights to the Scots; nor would they accept a plan put forward by the King's government – the Great Contract – by which, in return for a regular revenue, the King promised to give up all feudal dues belonging to the Crown and not to levy new impositions without the consent of the Commons. Faced by this opposition, James dissolved his first Parliament in February 1611.

In May 1612 Salisbury died, worn out in the King's service, for though James was willing enough to take decisions, he spent most of his daylight hours hunting stags and falling off horses in the process, while Salisbury had done all the hard work. After Salisbury's death, power came into the hands of royal favourites. James had married Princess Anne of Denmark in 1589 while he was the King of the Scots; he had romantically braved the perils of the Baltic in order to meet his wife at Oslo on her way to Scotland. They had six children, two sons, Henry and Charles, and four daughters, two of whom died very young. But basically James was homosexual and grew bored with the frivolity and stupidity of his Queen. His first favourite in England was a Scotsman, Robert Carr, who rose to power in 1610 and in 1613 was married with James's connivance to Frances Howard, daughter of the Earl of Suffolk, after her marriage to the third Earl of Essex was annulled. (Her father was to succeed Salisbury as Lord Treasurer.) But in 1616 Carr, who had been created Earl of Somerset and was made Lord Chamberlain, and his wife were accused of poisoning a former secretary of Somerset while he was imprisoned in the Tower of London. Though both were found guilty neither was severely punished, but Somerset's influence at court came to an abrupt end. James's next favourite was George Villiers who rose rapidly in the King's esteem and in 1623 was created Duke of Buckingham. During the last years of the reign Buckingham's influence on policy, particularly foreign policy, was decisive.

Go to the wars.

Aug. 26

English woodcutting entitled 'Go to the Wars'. It is taken from a pamphlet, *c.* 1619, depicting the resolution of London women to send their husbands to fight in the Thirty Years War, which raged across Europe during the reign of James I.

*Opposite*: Robert Carr, first Earl of Somerset, was the first favourite of James I and rose to the position of Lord Chamberlain. However, his influence over the King ended in 1616 when he was accused of poisoning a former secretary.

Although it was James's avowed intention to be a prince of peace, much of the remainder of the reign was absorbed in foreign affairs. In February 1613 his eldest daughter, Elizabeth, was married to Frederick the Elector Palatine who was a Calvinist and prominent among the German Protestant Princes. James himself entered into an alliance with the German Protestant Union and regarded himself as a Protestant

A study of George Villiers, Duke of Buckingham, by Peter Paul Rubens. As one of James I's favoured circle, he came to have a great influence on policy-making and encouraged the King into war with Spain.

champion. But at the same time he was anxious for an agreement with Spain, a country then regarded as the strongest in Europe. He aimed to reach an understanding by marrying his son Charles to the Spanish Infanta, sister of King Philip IV of Spain. He also put an end to his alliance with the Dutch, soon to renew their war against Spain, by selling back to them the towns acquired by Queen Elizabeth I.

In 1619 his son-in-law the Elector Palatine accepted the throne of Bohemia offered him by the Bohemian Protestant leaders. This led to war against the Holy Roman Emperor who himself claimed to be the rightful holder of the Bohemian throne. Thus James became reluctantly and at first indirectly involved in what was to be known as the Thirty Years' War in Germany, in which the Spaniards engaged on the side of the Emperor against the Elector Palatine who lost his hereditary throne. So James's foreign policy fell to pieces. Nevertheless he hoped that if the Spanish marriage alliance could be achieved he might persuade the Spanish government to use its influence with the Holy Roman Emperor to conclude a peaceable settlement with his son-in-law. But

James I swearing to the Spanish marriage treaty. James wanted his son Charles to marry the Spanish Infanta to create greater understanding between the two countries.

*Following pages*: 'The Life of Buckingham', by the nineteenth-century painter Augustus Egg, depicts the lavish extravagance of the court of James I.

this elaborate manoeuvre was doomed to failure and on Buckingham's instigation James was forced into a war with Spain and into hiring a mercenary army to fight against the Emperor.

Even before this James had grave financial difficulties. For he was grossly extravagant, spending, for example, a small fortune on his daughter's wedding, besides being lavish to his male favourites. When his second Parliament had met in 1614 he had vainly tried to persuade the Commons to vote him money, but the members expressed many grievances, especially over James's Scottish favourites, so that he was obliged to dissolve Parliament after two months. His third Parliament, which met in 1621, though avid for a war against Spain, thought that such a war should pay for itself and again demanded to discuss grievances before voting supplies. James said that foreign policy and religion were his business; when the Commons entered a protestation in its journal James tore the protestation out of the book and gave the order for the arrest of three or four of its leading members.

James employed various expedients other than impositions to raise money. Lionel Cranfield, the Earl of Middlesex, was appointed Lord Treasurer and reorganised the royal finances; Sir Walter Raleigh, one of Queen Elizabeth's favourites, was allowed to seek a mythical gold mine in Guiana; James granted commercial 'monopolies' from which Buckingham and his relatives largely profited; and he still hoped to procure money through his son's marriage. But he allowed his ablest servants to be dismissed and punished. His talented Lord Chancellor, Francis Bacon, was deprived of all his offices for taking bribes; Raleigh was put to death for conspiracy; and Middlesex was impeached by the Commons after Buckingham was convinced that the Lord Treasurer had failed him. So James's reign ended in confusion and disaster both at home and abroad.

Though James's mental capacities declined towards the end of his life, he was a highly intelligent ruler who did not provoke his leading subjects too far and was ready to withdraw unpopular policies. He was a learned theologian and after an original belief in witchcraft was persuaded finally of its falsity. But he was vain, lazy and too fond of his own voice. He allowed himself to be increasingly imposed upon by male favourites while 'he piqued himself on his great contempt for women'. Before he died on 27 March 1625 he recognised the growing influence of the House of Commons and vainly warned his heir of the dangers that awaited him.

*Opposite:* Portrait of Francis Bacon. A talented Lord Chancellor, Bacon was dismissed from office by James I for taking bribes.

# CHARLES I *r.* 1625-49

THE SECOND SON OF JAMES I and Anne of Denmark was born in Dunfermline Palace, twelve miles from Edinburgh, on 19 November 1600. Charles was a weak and backward child and needed the permission of the royal doctors to be brought south in a curtained litter after his father settled in England. Like his father he was educated by a Scottish Presbyterian tutor, mastered Latin and Greek and showed an aptitude for modern languages. His brother Henry, who was six years his elder and whom Charles admired, died in 1612 when he was eighteen. In the following year Charles's sister Elizabeth departed with her husband for Heidelberg. Thus the shy and reserved boy – he never overcame a stammer – was created Prince of Wales in 1616, becoming important but lonely. In 1619 his mother died, but he struck up a friendship with the Marquis of Buckingham, his father's favourite, while James himself proved a conscientious and loving father. By 1624, going with Buckingham on an incognito mission to Madrid in search of a Spanish wife, Charles was described as having 'grown into a fine gentleman'. He was five feet four inches tall. The flattering portraits of him by Van Dyck and Bower made him appear more dignified than he really was. In fact he was a small man who in due course enjoyed asserting himself.

On 27 March 1625 Charles succeeded to the throne and within two months was married to Henrietta Maria, the sister of King Louis XIII of France. When in Madrid Charles had been attracted by the languorous Spanish Princess, who shrank from him as a heretic; at first he thought his French wife disappointing and took a dislike to her train of priests and women she brought over with her from Paris, some of

*Opposite*: The young Duke of York, later Charles I, painted by Robert Peake. He was a sickly child, yet it was his brother Henry, six years his senior, who died prematurely, leaving Charles as heir to their father's throne.

The Highe and Mightie Prince FREDERICK the fift by the grace of God Counte Palatine of Rheyn Duke of Bavier Elector and Arch-Sewer of the Sacred Romane Empire and is vicaire of the same Vicar therof And Knight of the most noble order of the Garter. Borne 1596. | The most excelent Princesse ELIZABETH th'onely Daughter to our Soueraigne Lord Iames King of Great Brittaine France and Ireland &c. Borne the 19 of August 1596. Maried the 14 of Februarie 1612.

Prince Frederick, Elector Palatine, and Elizabeth, Queen of Bohemia. Elizabeth was the eldest daughter of James I and her marriage to the German Protestant prince was part of James's scheme of championing the Protestant cause in Europe.

*Following pages:* King Charles I with his wife, Queen Henrietta Maria, about to depart for the chase.

whom he sent packing. For the first years of his reign he was under the influence of Buckingham and found himself at war with both Spain and France. The expeditions against these countries organised and on occasion led by Buckingham were complete failures. Because of their distrust of Buckingham the House of Commons refused to grant Charles the supplies he needed to wage wars, while even the Customs duties (known then as tonnage and poundage) were voted for his use only for a single year. So Charles was driven to a number of financial

*Opposite:* Cornelius Johnson's portrait of Henrietta Maria, the sister of King Louis XIII of France who married Charles I in the year of his coronation. His initial indifference turned to love after the death of the Duke of Buckingham, under whose powerful influence he, like his father, found himself.

A gold three pound coin depicting Charles I, minted in Oxford during 1644.

*Following pages*: 'The children of Charles I of England' by van Dyck, 1637. Depicted are the future Kings Charles II and James II and Princesses Mary, Elizabeth and Anne.

*Opposite*: King Charles I out hunting by van Dyck, *c*. 1635. Charles was only five feet four inches tall and many of van Dyck's flattering portraits make him more dignified than he actually was.

expedients; he cashed his wife's dowry; he exacted forced loans from his wealthier subjects, imprisoning five knights who refused to pay; he billeted soldiers without paying for them; and he collected tonnage and poundage without Parliamentary sanction. Both the Parliaments of 1625 and 1626 showed their distrust of the King and Buckingham.

When Charles's third Parliament met in 1628, after the failure of the campaigns against Spain, the leading Members of the Commons were extremely critical of the government. Not only did they resent the royal financial methods but they complained about the mismanagement of the war against the Spaniards and on behalf of the French Protestants, and also objected to the King's attitude to the Church of England. For although Charles had been tutored by a Scottish Calvinist, he was a man of fastidious tastes who disliked the kind of church services of which the Puritans most approved. He was accused of promoting so-called 'Arminians' or high churchmen who believed in free will rather than predestination to achieve salvation and of appointing clergy who preferred the retention of Catholic ritual and rites in services to long sermons and extempore prayer.

The Commons showed themselves extremely restless; a Petition of Rights was drawn up with the concurrence of the House of Lords in which forced loans, the billeting of soldiers, the imprisonment of subjects without cause shown, and other grievances were condemned. Charles accepted the petition with reluctance, but scarcely abided by it. When the Commons went on to condemn the King's favourite divines and to threaten the impeachment of his friend Buckingham, Charles felt obliged to adjourn Parliament without obtaining the money he needed from it.

The assassination of Buckingham by a fanatic in August 1628 failed to reconcile Charles with his Parliament. Before he again adjourned it in March 1629 the Speaker of the Commons was held down in his chair while resolutions were unanimously passed condemning 'innovations' in religion and the illegal levying of tonnage and poundage. For the next eleven years Charles governed without Parliament and saved money by bringing the wars to an end. In 1633, however, he appointed a leading

Three children of Charles I: James, Duke of York (centre), Princess Elizabeth (left) and Prince Henry (right).

Arminian, William Laud, as Archbishop of Canterbury and with his aid set out to impose a service book drawn up in London on the Scottish Church or Kirk so that the religious practices of his two kingdoms should become uniform. Provoked by this action the Scottish lowlanders turned against their King and swore to uphold a National Covenant embodying loyalty to the Kirk, as exemplified in the public rejection of the new service book. Infuriated by this rebelliousness, Charles raised an army to enforce his wishes on Scotland. He was humiliatingly rebuffed in what was known as the first Bishops' War. To pay for a second campaign he was compelled to summon a new Parliament at Westminster.

This Parliament insisted on discussing their pent-up grievances before voting the King money. So Charles dissolved it after a few weeks, which gave it the sobriquet of 'the Short Parliament'. For a second time Charles sent an army against his Scottish subjects; this time he was conclusively beaten. The King was thus obliged to pay the Covenanter army while it was encamped on English soil in Northumberland and Durham and again threw himself on the mercy of an English Parliament, which met in November 1640 and was to be called the Long Parliament.

During the long interval before the Short and Long Parliaments met, the King's government had employed a number of dubious methods of raising money. 'Ship money', a tax which had been used in Tudor times, was imposed on inland towns as well as ports to pay for the upkeep of the navy. Tonnage and poundage continued to be levied illegally. Various irritating medieval imposts, such as fines upon gentry who refused to accept knighthoods, were collected. Thus the whole of

The Lower House of Parliament assembled at Westminster on 13 April 1640. Around the outside are the plans of the 38 towns represented in parliament.

Three views of the head of Charles I, painted by van Dyck to assist the sculptor Bernini to complete a bust of the King, which has since been lost.

the House of Commons, consisting of country gentlemen, lawyers and merchants, were alienated from the King's government which they considered to be acting unconstitutionally. Fears grew that the English army in the north and the garrison of Ireland were going to be employed to enforce the King's absolute will on Parliament. In fact Charles had no intention of doing anything of the sort, but his ablest minister, the Earl of Strafford, Lord Lieutenant of Ireland, whom he had summoned to organise the second Bishops' War, was selected by the Commons as a scapegoat. They reckoned him with Archbishop Laud as the chief of the King's 'evil counsellors' and it was decided to impeach Strafford for treason before the House of Lords.

Charles understood what the Commons had in mind. But he hoped that if Strafford defended himself successfully before his fellow peers the whole absolutist system of government, called by its opponents 'the eleven years' tyranny', would be vindicated. However, when the trial for treason faltered, Charles was asked to sign a Bill of Attainder by which Strafford could be put to death without any legal judgement. The King was subjected to heavy pressures; the House of Lords was menaced by city mobs; the King believed that his Roman Catholic Queen, with whom he had fallen in love since the death of Buckingham, was in peril. Reluctantly he signed the Bill. Afterwards he gave way over ship money and agreed that this Long Parliament should not be dissolved without its own consent.

Only on two questions did Charles refuse to yield to the pressure of the leaders of Parliament. The first was over the reform of the Church of England, which they held was being catholicised by the King's High Church bishops; the second was over the control of the militia, the only permanent armed force in the kingdom apart from the King's own guards. In the summer of 1641 Charles visited Scotland in the hope that by offering concessions to his subjects there he could rally them to the defence of the throne. When he returned empty-handed from Scotland, he found that about half the Members of the Commons were now veering towards his side. A Grand Remonstrance, which set out all the grievances against his government, was only carried by a few votes in November. Egged on by his Queen, the King now attempted to arrest five leading Members of the Commons, including his chief critic, John Pym. But when he entered the House in January 1642 he discovered that 'the birds had flown'. He then left London and both sides – the Royalists and the Parliamentarians – prepared for civil war.

During the next seven months negotiations went on between the two parties for a peace treaty. But they broke down on the two principal questions over which the King was willing to compromise but not to yield. Parliament also demanded the right to nominate all his ministers and military officers, even to supervise the upbringing of his children. Gradually hopes of a peaceful settlement faded; and the first civil war began when Charles raised his standard at Nottingham on 22 August 1642.

Charles had many fine qualities. He was temperate and grave, a devoted husband and father, and a sincere Christian. He was an aesthete who spent money on beautiful things. Inigo Jones, to be famous as an architect, and Ben Jonson, the playwright, designed masques for the court; Rubens was brought over to England to paint the ceiling of the

A drawing of Inigo Jones by
van Dyck. Jones, later famous
as an architect, was one of
the many artists who enjoyed
the patronage of Charles I.

banqueting house in Whitehall Palace in memory of Charles's father. Van
Dyck did portraits of the royal family, and other artists, such as William
Dobson, an outstanding native portrait painter, enjoyed the King's
patronage. But Charles also had serious defects. He was lazy and lacked
any sense of humour. Moreover he thought any means were justified to
win the war and regain his absolute authority. Consequently he made
all sorts of contradictory promises to Scottish Presbyterians, English
Anglicans, Irish Roman Catholics and the Puritan leaders of the
Parliamentary army, which he had no intention of keeping. Gradually
he forfeited all trust.

As commander-in-chief of the army which he raised with difficulty from among his loyal subjects to fight Parliament, he was by no means negligible as a tactician. He distinguished himself at the battle of Edgehill in 1642, at Cropredy Bridge and Lostwithiel in 1644 and at the relief of Hereford in 1645. But as a strategist he constantly vacillated. He refused to march on London after Edgehill or when his fortunes were high in 1643. He failed to impose his will on his generals. Towards the end he could not decide whether to fight in England or to join his supporters in Scotland. Eventually, after major defeats, he resolved to leave his headquarters at Oxford in disguise and make for the camp of the Scottish Covenanter army which had allied itself with the English Parliamentarians and conquered the north-east of England. As he refused to promise to introduce the full Presbyterian system of Church government in England, the Covenanters handed him over to the

The costumes designed for King Charles and Queen Henrietta Maria by Inigo Jones to be worn in the masque *Salmacida Spolia* in 1640. In such masques the court presented itself in an idealised way, offering images of the king and queen that bore little relation to political situation.

THE ROYALL OAKE OF BRITTAYNE

An engraving from 1651 of the symbolic Royal Oak Tree being destroyed in the Civil War under the guidance of Oliver Cromwell, showing the royal arms, the crown and the royal sword, Magna Carta, the Statutes of Parliament and the Bible itself.

*Opposite:* Oliver Cromwell by Sir Peter Lely. Cromwell emerged from the Civil Wars as leader of the Puritan faction in Parliament and ruled England as Lord Protector and Head of State from 1653 until his death in 1659.

English Parliament, but in 1647 he fell into the hands of the victorious Roundhead army led by Thomas Fairfax and Oliver Cromwell.

Both Fairfax and Cromwell were anxious to come to terms with the King on the basis of a written constitution, in which the King's authority could be harmonised with the wishes of his leading subjects. A scheme drawn up by the army commanders known as the Heads of the Proposals was considered by some of Charles's advisers to be a cheap way of regaining authority after his defeat.

But rather than come to an agreed settlement Charles preferred trying to play off his enemies against each other. He escaped from honourable captivity in Hampton Court and fled to the Isle of Wight; thence he bargained both with the Parliamentarians, among whom there was a substantial peace party, and with his Scottish subjects, who did not care for the imprisonment of a Stuart king by the English and

OLIVER   *Lely. fe*   CROMWELL. P.

were ready to engage themselves in his service in return for mainly religious concessions. Charles accepted this 'engagement'; the Scottish 'engagers' invaded England in 1648 while earlier in the same year many Royalists, tired of Puritan restraints and exactions, took up arms again. The second civil war was quickly over. Cromwell defeated the Scots and left a garrison in Edinburgh; Fairfax overcame the Royalist revolt in south-eastern England. Though part of the navy deserted the Parliamentarians for the King, it did not even attempt to rescue him from imprisonment in the Isle of Wight.

The army leaders determined that the King should be put on trial for waging war on his own people. The House of Commons was purged of the peace party which had vainly negotiated with Charles in the Isle of Wight. A high court of justice was erected and the King

The trial of King Charles I. The decision to try the King was made by a minority of members after the army had purged Parliament. The King refused to recognise the legality of the trial and made no defence.

The Tryal of the King.

The Army having purg'd the House of Commons, and left none but their own Creatures to sit there, appointed a Committee for y
Kings Tryal w^h began 20 Jan: 1648, on which day 67 Commissioners were present and when Gen^l Fairfax's Name was called over his
Lady cryed out He has more Wit than to be here, and when he was Indited in the Name of all the good People of England she also cry
ed out, no nor one hundred part of them, his Gold Head dropt from his Cane, this day without any visible cause, on the 2^d 70 Commis
sioners were present, as were 71 on the 3^d day, and 66 on the 4^th when Bradshaw pronounced the Sentence.

brought to Westminster Hall in January 1649 to face his trial. The King conducted himself with dignity, refusing to recognise the legality of the court and thus making no real defence. The court condemned him to death. On 30 January 1649 he was publicly executed outside Whitehall Palace and his body was secretly buried in Windsor Castle.

A contemporary German print depicting the public execution of King Charles I on 30 January 1649.

# CHARLES II *r.* 1660-85

THE ELDEST SURVIVING SON OF Charles I and Henrietta Maria was born on 29 May 1630 and sealed his father's and mother's newly found married happiness. He was brought up as a child in that idealistic atmosphere which was pictured by Van Dyck and described by the Earl of Clarendon in his celebrated *History*, before the clouds which heralded the civil wars began to gather. His first governor was the wealthy and cultivated magnifico, the second Earl of Newcastle, who told him that he would learn more from men than books. He was only twelve when the civil war began and was present at the first big battle, Edgehill. Two years later he accompanied his father on his victorious campaign in Cornwall, and in March 1645 Charles I sent him, when only fourteen, to be nominal commander-in-chief in western England with his headquarters at Bristol.

After being driven for a year from pillar to post by the conquering Parliamentarians, he was forced to leave England together with his Council (which included some able men) first for the Scillies, then Jersey, and finally, on his father's orders, he joined his mother in Paris. In 1648 he took command of the warships which had mutinied against Parliament during the second civil war, but was obliged to return to his base in Holland where at the beginning of 1649 he learned of his father's execution. The next eleven years he devoted to trying to gain the thrones of England and Scotland.

Charles arrived in Scotland in 1650 where he was humiliatingly treated by the bigoted Covenanters. However, after Cromwell's victory at Dunbar, his stock rose; he was crowned King of the Scots and allowed to take command of a united Scottish army. In the summer of 1651 he

*Opposite*: Bust-length portrait of King Charles II wearing the robes of the Order of the Garter, by an artist from the circle of Sir Peter Lely.

Charles 2<sup>nd</sup>

led this army into England only to be conclusively defeated by Cromwell at the battle of Worcester, where he fought extremely bravely. He escaped from the field of battle and after many exciting adventures managed to return safely to France. Next year the first war between England and the Dutch Republic broke out. Charles vainly offered his services to the Dutch and later when Spain was at war with England he succeeded in concluding a treaty of alliance in Brussels which promised that if the Royalists could lay hold of a port in England he would be provided with an expeditionary army. Nothing came of his plans. It was not until after the death of Oliver Cromwell, which was followed by anarchic struggles between Oliver's would-be successors, that Charles was by general acclamation welcomed back to England. He arrived in London on his thirtieth birthday.

Charles had been extremely skilful in the way in which he seized this opportunity. In his Declaration of Breda (4 April 1660) he did not commit himself to any specific undertakings about a constitutional settlement except that he promised 'liberty of conscience' to all Christians and demanded the punishment of his father's murderers. In fact he was relatively merciful, and made earnest efforts to achieve an agreement between the enthusiastic supporters of the old Church of England and the Presbyterians who had helped to procure his restoration. However, negotiations broke down. A new prayer book was drawn up; an Act of Uniformity was passed; and some 2,000 clergy left their parishes. Moreover Charles's second Parliament, elected in May 1661, refused to accept a Declaration of Indulgence which he issued and for a time showed itself to be more rigidly Anglican than the King.

Charles had been crowned on 23 April 1661 and a year later he was married to Catherine of Braganza, the daughter of the King of Portugal. His ministers were chiefly the old Royalists who had served him during his long exile from England together with General George Monck, the

The return of Charles II to England, from a prayer book *c.* 1660. Charles entered London on his thirtieth birthday after the political struggles that followed the death of Cromwell in 1659.

*Opposite:* The future Charles II aged twelve at the battle of Edgehill in 1642. He played an active role during the Civil Wars and in 1645 Charles I placed him in nominal command of Royalist forces in western England.

man chiefly responsible for the Restoration, who was created Duke of Albemarle. In 1665 the House of Commons pressurised Charles into a war with the Dutch over which he was not at all keen and the causes of which were largely naval and commercial rivalries. Though the King had inherited a big navy from the Cromwellian period, the Dutch more than held their own. The reason for their success was not that Charles lacked good admirals but that the kingdom was distracted first by the Great Plague and then by the Great Fire in London. Furthermore naval warfare was expensive and the Commons did not vote enough money to wage a long war. In July 1667 a peace was concluded which left the position much as it was before the war. Nevertheless the leading subjects of the King were disappointed and to appease

Huych Allaerdt Exc.

*Opposite:* Coin minted in 1662 to commemorate the marriage of King Charles II and Catherine of Braganza, daughter of the King of Portugal.

*Following pages:* Contemporary Dutch painting depicting the Great Fire of London of 1666. The disastrous fire was one of several domestic issues that distracted Charles from the prosecution of war against the Dutch.

General George Monck, who was chiefly responsible for the restoration of the monarchy under Charles II. For his services the new King raised Monck to the peerage as the Duke of Albemarle.

them Charles dismissed his chief minister, Edward Hyde, Earl of Clarendon. A group of five men now became the King's closest advisers: Lord Clifford, Lord Arlington, the Duke of Buckingham, Lord Ashley and Lord Lauderdale, known as 'the Cabal', the word formed by the first letters of their names.

The next few years were dominated by questions of foreign policy. Charles decided that he must have his revenge on the Dutch. Though for a time he entered upon a Protestant alliance with the Dutch and the Swedes, he was resolved to become the ally of the French monarchy

*Opposite:* The coronation of Charles II as King of Scotland took place at the Scone palace in 1650. He invaded England in 1651, was defeated at Worcester and fled to safety in France.

A Representation of the Popish Plott in 29 figures, as y manner of killing St Edmond bury Godfry, & their horid designes to kill the King, and the manner of the Plotters Execution.

Sold by Robert Greene. at the Rose and Crowne in Budge Rowe.

The Plott first hached at Rome by the Pope and Cardinalls.

London remember the 2d of Septr. 1666.

Sr E.B. Godfry takeing Dr Oates his depositions.

Dr Oates discovers the Plott to y King & Councel.

Sr E.B.Godfry strangled Girald going to stab him.

The dead body of Sr E.B Godfry conveyd out of Somerset house in a Sedan.

The body of Sr E.B.G. conveyd to Primrose hill on a Hors.

The Funerall of Sr Edmond bury Godfry.

Prance discovers y murther of Sr E.B.Godfry to the King and Counsell.

The Execution of y murderers of Sr Edmond bury Godfry.

Coleman giveth a Guiny to incourage y 4 Ruffians.

The Irish Ruffians going for Windsor.

Pickerin attempts to kill y King in St James P.

Coleman writing a declaration and Letters to la Chess

Capt Bedlom carrying Letters to forrain parts

Redding endevoring to corrupt Capt Bedlow.

Redding standing in the pillory.

Mr Everard imprison'd in the Tower.

The Execution of the 5 Iesuits.

Ashby receiv'd instruction of Whitebread for the society to offer St George Wakeman an 10000

Ireland and Grove drawn to their Execution

Coleman drawn to his Execution.

Sr Willm Waller burning Popish books and Images

Pickering Executed.

Gifford and Stubs gives mony to a Maid to fire her Masters house.

Capt Berry and Alderman Brooks are offered god to cast y Plot on the Protestants.

Mr Dugdale in Staffordshire reading severall letters relating to the Plott.

Whitebread made Provintiall.

The Lord Stafford Beheading.

which had become the strongest single power in Europe. After complicated negotiations in which Charles's youngest sister, Henrietta, played an important part, a secret treaty was signed at Dover in May 1670. By this treaty Charles undertook to wage war against the Dutch together with the French, while by a secret clause he promised to declare himself at an appropriate time to be Roman Catholic. The French undertook to pay him financial subsidies and, when the war had been won, to award him Dutch ports. The treaty was concealed from Charles's dedicated Protestant ministers of state such as Anthony Ashley Cooper, Earl of Shaftesbury. One of his Catholic ministers, Lord Clifford, offered by hook or by crook to raise the money necessary to fight the war even if the House of Commons refused. To keep his promise to the French King about helping the English Catholics, Charles published a second Declaration of Indulgence; then, without Parliament being informed, the war began.

Although the French army overran much of the Dutch Republic the English navy was kept away from the Dutch coasts; the intention

*Opposite:* A 'history' of the 1678 'Popish Plot' to murder Charles II and install James as King. Charles was unable to keep the anti-papacy frenzy under control and twenty-four Catholics were executed.

Pamphlet printed for Langley Curtis. On the left are two kings kneeling before the Pope, with London burning in the background, the poisoning of Charles II, the body of a loyal courtier lying in a field and the martyrdom of English bishops. On the right are Charles II with a representation of the church at his feet and the executions of traitors in the background.

# BABEL and BETHEL: or, The POPE in his Colours.

WITH

The Church of *ENGLAND*'s Supplication to his Majesty, our gracious Soveraign, the true Defender of the Faith; To protect her from all the Machinations of *Rome*, and its bloody Emissaries.

*Rome's Scarlet whore doth here in Tryumph Ride;*
*And Spurns off Soveraign Crowns in height of Pride*
*Poor Christians and brave Citties too shee Burns*
*And Stabbs and Poisons daily serve her Turns.*

*Behold our Church (like Esther here doth tend)*
*Her Supplication to the Faiths Defender*
*In vain Rome Plots, while Charles's Scepter Sways*
*May bleed and Gibbet end all Traitors Days.*

Scarce had *bright Truth*, with an enliv'ning Ray,
Chac'd the *black Mists* of Ignorance away,
Restor'd the *Gospel*, and our Souls set free

*Two Swords* are brandisht in his bloody hand,
Boasting both *Souls* and *Bodies* to Command;
The double *Engines* of his fatal Ills;

"Let not *Zerviah's brood* too strong become,
"But scatter all th'Intrigues of *bloody ROME.*
This said ——

had been to land an expeditionary force to aid the French. The House of Commons showed itself to be increasingly anti-French and anti-Catholic. Charles was asked to withdraw his Declaration of Indulgence and to agree to a Test Act excluding Roman Catholics from all offices. Though the King did so, he was refused the money he needed to continue the war and so he was compelled to make a separate peace. The next five years were concerned mainly with foreign affairs. Charles tried to act as a mediator between the Dutch and the French, though he was still drawing subsidies from the French King, while the Commons vigorously demanded that he should go to war with France. In the end he was driven to agree to a marriage between Prince William III of Orange, the Dutch Captain-General, and his niece Mary, and to threaten war against France. But his actions had small influence upon the Peace of Nymegen which ended the war in 1678.

In the course of these years Charles had managed to raise a small army; Parliament became afraid that he was aiming at absolutism, though that was not his intention at this stage of his reign. Domestic affairs became difficult for him as an anti-Catholic agitation boiled up. His brother James, Duke of York, was now known to be a Roman Catholic convert because he had resigned all his offices after the passing of the first Test Act; he then married a Roman Catholic Italian princess as his second wife; the Queen was also a Roman Catholic, as was Charles's principal mistress, the French Duchess of Portsmouth; and suspicions arose over what Charles had promised the French by treaty. In the summer of 1678 a 'Popish Plot' was revealed to the government by perjured informers. Charles insisted that the whole plot was 'a contrivance'. But when the Duchess of York's secretary, named Coleman, was arrested and incriminating letters found outlining Roman Catholic aspirations, Charles was unable to keep the general frenzy under control. Coleman and a number of Jesuits were put to death. The Earl of Danby, who became Lord Treasurer and the King's chief minister when the Cabal broke up in 1674, was threatened with impeachment and the Commons were angered by revelations about Charles's pro-French policy for which in fact Danby had not been responsible. In January 1679 Charles dissolved the former Cavalier Parliament which had sat for eighteen years. Before its dissolution a second Test Act was passed excluding Roman Catholics from sitting in either House of Parliament.

When a new Parliament met in the spring a Bill to exclude the Duke of York from succession to the throne was introduced. Charles,

*Opposite*: Portrait of Mol Davies, by Sir Peter Lely. Davies was one of a succession of mistresses taken by Charles II to satisfy his voracious sexual appetite.

now virtually his own first minister, was determined to prevent its enactment. For two years a contest took place between the King's supporters, the Tories, and their opponents, the Whigs, who were led by the unscrupulous Shaftesbury. Charles stopped the passage of an Exclusion Bill by bringing his own influence to bear on the House of Lords. In 1680 the fourth Parliament of the reign met and again the Commons voted for exclusion. Charles dissolved it. In 1681 he summoned a fifth Parliament to meet in Oxford where he exerted military pressure upon the Whigs. He and his brother were now genuinely afraid of civil war, but the King kept his head. He came to a secret understanding with the French King that he would be given support in the event of a rebellion. A Tory reaction slowly set in, aided by the revelation of what was called 'the Rye House plot', an alleged conspiracy to murder the King on his way from the Newcastle races, engineered by the Whigs. By using his influence to obtain friendly officials in key posts both in the government and in the counties, the King succeeded in crushing the Whig movement and its leaders fled abroad. Shaftesbury died in Holland. The last four years of Charles's reign were peaceable. He had enough money to live on because of the expansion of the receipts from the Customs and Excise, and he had an army on which he could rely. His Roman Catholic brother in effect resumed his post as Lord High Admiral.

Charles thus proved himself an extremely shrewd politician as well as a ready liar. Though like his father and grandfather he was rather lazy, he could exert himself effectively at times of crisis. With the exception of the two Test Acts he made few concessions to Parliament. Like his father he refused to give up control over the armed forces of the kingdom; unlike him, he saved his leading ministers from execution for treason. Charles had charm and a vast sense of humour which caused him to be much loved by ordinary people. The 'Merry Monarch' did not eat or drink to excess but he had a large sexual appetite, enjoying a succession of mistresses – Nell Gwynne is the best remembered – whom he rewarded generously but did not love. He refused to divorce the Queen, though she could bear him no children. His main interest was the navy, but he also enjoyed horse races and fishing. He was very human and, from the point of view of his dynasty, a successful king. Before he died on 6 February 1685 he was received into the Roman Catholic Church, but there is considerable evidence that even before his restoration he had been a Catholic at heart. He was buried in Westminster Abbey.

*Opposite*: Nell Gwynne's portrait, from the studio of Sir Peter Lely. She rose from selling oranges on the street to become a leading actress of the day and the most famous of Charles II's mistresses.

# JAMES II *r.* 1685–8

THE SECOND SON OF CHARLES I, James, Duke of York, was only twelve (he was born on 14 October 1633) when the City of Oxford, in which he had been raised, surrendered to the Parliamentarians and the Prince himself was taken as a prisoner to St James's Palace in London. In April 1648 he managed to escape dressed as a girl and found his way to his sister Mary in Holland. After his father's execution he was appointed Lord High Admiral by his brother, but Charles II refused to let him sail with the fleet. Instead James was commissioned as an officer in the French army. By the time he was twenty-one he had been promoted to lieutenant-general. He distinguished himself as a soldier, and his conduct was commended by the famous French marshal Turenne. But when the French government came to terms with the Cromwellian Protectorate James reluctantly resigned his commission. Instead he served with the Spaniards, who were fighting the French and the English republicans in 1658. That June in the battle of the Dunes James again fought courageously and thus by the time that his brother was restored to the English throne James had earned a high reputation as a soldier.

Two occurrences, which were kept secret before the Restoration, were that James had been attracted to the Roman Catholic Church and that he had signed a contract of marriage with Anne Hyde, the daughter of the future Earl of Clarendon who had been the Chancellor of Charles II's Exchequer and was afterwards Lord Chancellor. Charles II insisted that his brother should publicly acknowledge the marriage. James took an active part in Charles's counsels and when the first Anglo-Dutch war of the new reign broke out he commanded the navy in person, inflicting a defeat on the Dutch at the battle of Lowestoft in

*Opposite*: James II succeeded his brother surprisingly peacefully given his open allegiance to Roman Catholicism, but his reign was to be a brief one.

ANN DVTCHESS OF
YORK

June 1665. But the King refused to let him go to sea again until the second war of the reign. Then he was in the thick of the battle of Solebay, fought in May 1672, but, though assisted by a French squadron, failed to defeat the Dutch who were determined to prevent enemy troops landing from the sea.

James's conversion to the Roman Church took place in 1668, but he continued to attend Anglican services for another eight years. When the first Test Act was carried he felt constrained to resign his post as Lord High Admiral, but consoled himself by his second marriage, to the young Mary of Modena. As the anti-Catholic agitation, which culminated in the disclosure of the 'Popish Plot', was intensified, he became the target of the Whigs' wrath. They aimed to exclude him from succession to the throne and Charles sent James into exile first in Brussels and then in Edinburgh to allow tempers to cool. It was not until the Tory reaction set in that the King allowed his brother to return to Whitehall. This was in 1682 when the Duke brought an action for libel against Titus Oates, the fountain-head of the Popish Plot. During the last three years of Charles II's reign James served in the Privy Council and on the Committee for Foreign Affairs and in effect resumed his position as Lord High Admiral. Sir John Reresby noted in January 1682 that 'the Duke of York did chiefly manage affairs, but with great haughtiness'.

When Charles II died in February 1685 James succeeded to the throne unexpectedly peacefully considering the attempts that the Commons had made to exclude him because he was an avowed Roman Catholic. He at once openly attended Mass, but informed the Privy Council and a new Parliament which met in May 1685 that he would protect the Church of England 'whose members have shown themselves so eminently loyal in the worst of times'. The House of Commons consisted for the most part of members who were strongly

See here the Devils Darling, plotting still
With Blood & Treasons all y̅ world to fill,
His Romish stratagems, Loe, Non can tell
Popes. Who canot fathom to y̅ Depth of Hell.
Nothing but Murder'd Kings can him suffice
And flaming Citys as a Sacrifice

Yet see behind his chaire Whom Heav'n sent,
Whom God hath made a timely Instrument
England's intended ruine to prevent
Oates. That which, y̅ Devil & y̅ Popes combin'd
Against our King and Protestants design'd

The Emblem Explayn'd

A.A. the Popes Cabbinett.
B. the Pope writing to the Jesuits to be diligent in the carueing on the Plott
C. m̅. Oate who unfsene takes ouer his sholder & sees all his Contriuance.
D. the Popes Crone who cries friend Oates is behind you .
E. the Popes title of Supremacie falling donne accusumed by his Iudaine Motion
F. a Blett in which his Perpryse made him fall upon y̅ word Roman in his Letter
G. a croune m̅. Oates giue a him more fitt for his Head then the former.

Contemporary English engraving of Titus Oates. He was partly responsible for exposing the 'Popish Plot' and is here portrayed as defending the liberties of England from Popery.

*Opposite*: Anne Hyde, first wife of James II. James signed a secret contract of marriage before the restoration of his brother; on taking the throne, Charles insisted that it should be publicly acknowledged.

The coronation of James II and his second wife, Mary of Modena, on 23 April 1685.

*Opposite:* A portrait of Mary of Modena, who was James's second wife and became Queen. He had previously signed a marriage contract with Anne Hyde, who bore him two daughters, Queen Mary II and Queen Anne.

Royalist and Anglican; it was determined to give James a fair trial as ruler and voted him a generous revenue. Nevertheless the King treated it superciliously and he was annoyed when a resolution was passed asking him to publish a proclamation to put in force the laws against 'all dissenters whatsoever from the Church of England'. For James's intention was precisely the opposite. He was determined to place both Roman Catholics and Protestant dissenters in a position of civic equality with his Anglican subjects.

In June 1685 Scotland was invaded by a rebel force directed by the Marquis of Argyll, while Charles II's eldest illegitimate son, the Duke of Monmouth, landed in the south-west of England. The two rebel leaders had assumed that their countries would refuse to obey a Roman Catholic king but the invasions were defeated without undue difficulty. Parliament showed its loyalty to James and during the summer harmony reigned. Yet by the autumn James's decision to allow Roman Catholic officers to serve in the army in spite of the first Test Act and his insistence on the suspension of the penal laws against nonconformists provoked the Commons to protest. They did not at all care for the idea of a standing army, recently victorious over Monmouth and officered by Catholics, being at the King's disposal. So this Parliament, initially

entirely loyal, became so restive that James prorogued it on 20 November 1685, though he did not dissolve it until July 1687. Thus he lost some of his promised revenue, but was able to exploit his royal prerogatives of suspending or dispensing with laws to pursue his policy of introducing complete religious equality.

The first thing he did was to appoint an ecclesiastical commission which was intended to prevent Anglican clergy from attacking the tenets of the Roman Catholic religion from their pulpits, which James called 'indiscreet preaching'. This commission proceeded to suspend the Bishop of London from his office because he disobeyed the King's orders. Next a test case was brought before the high court which decided (after the judges had been purged) that it was legal for James to dispense with the law in individual cases. This verdict enabled him to admit Roman Catholics into the Privy Council, freely to employ Roman Catholics as military and naval officers, and even to choose Catholics for positions in Oxford colleges. On 4 April 1687 he issued a Declaration of Indulgence aiming at complete religious toleration; a second Declaration was published a year later. The Anglican clergy were instructed to read it from their pulpits on the following Sundays. Finally James dismissed from office his two brothers-in-law, sons of Clarendon, who as Protestants did not altogether approve of his policies. The unscrupulous Earl of Sunderland then became Lord President of the Council as well as Secretary of State.

The summer of 1688 was the turning point in James's reign. The Archbishop of Canterbury and six other bishops petitioned the King to withdraw his orders about the second Declaration of Indulgence on the grounds that Parliaments of Charles II's reign had insisted that the King had no right to dispense with the penal code. James was furious and ordered that the seven bishops should be put on trial before the King's Bench for seditious libel. They were acquitted by a jury and the verdict was celebrated not only in the streets of London but even in the army camp at Hounslow. On 10 June the Queen gave birth to a son – to be known as the Old Pretender. Thus it seemed as if a Roman Catholic dynasty would become permanent. On the same day that the bishops were acquitted the Bishop of London and six laymen – to be called the Immortal Seven – secretly invited James's nephew and son-in-law, William of Orange, to come over to England to protect liberty and property and to sustain his wife's right to succeed to the throne since it was alleged (wrongly) that the birth of the Old Pretender was an imposture.

*Opposite*: 'The Old Pretender', James Edward Stuart, son of James II and Mary Modena. His birth appeared to secure a Catholic dynasty on the throne of England.

James R

Wee doe hereby graciously declare our continued sense of ye long & faythfull services performed to our late Dearest Brother & our selfe by Mr. Pepys our Secretary for ye Affayres of our Admiralty of England, & that his long want of Satisfaction to his just pretensions attested by our selfe when Duke of Yorke & confirmed by our sayd Dearest Brother in a state thereof bearing date ye second day of March 1678/9 shall bee noe impediment to his receiving ye same from us; wee hereby earnestly recommending him to ye Lords Comissrs of our Treasury for theyr doeing him full right on our behalfe therein, & in what is further due to him on his Account as late Treasurer for Tangier. Given at our Castle of Windsor this 17th day of November 1688.

JR

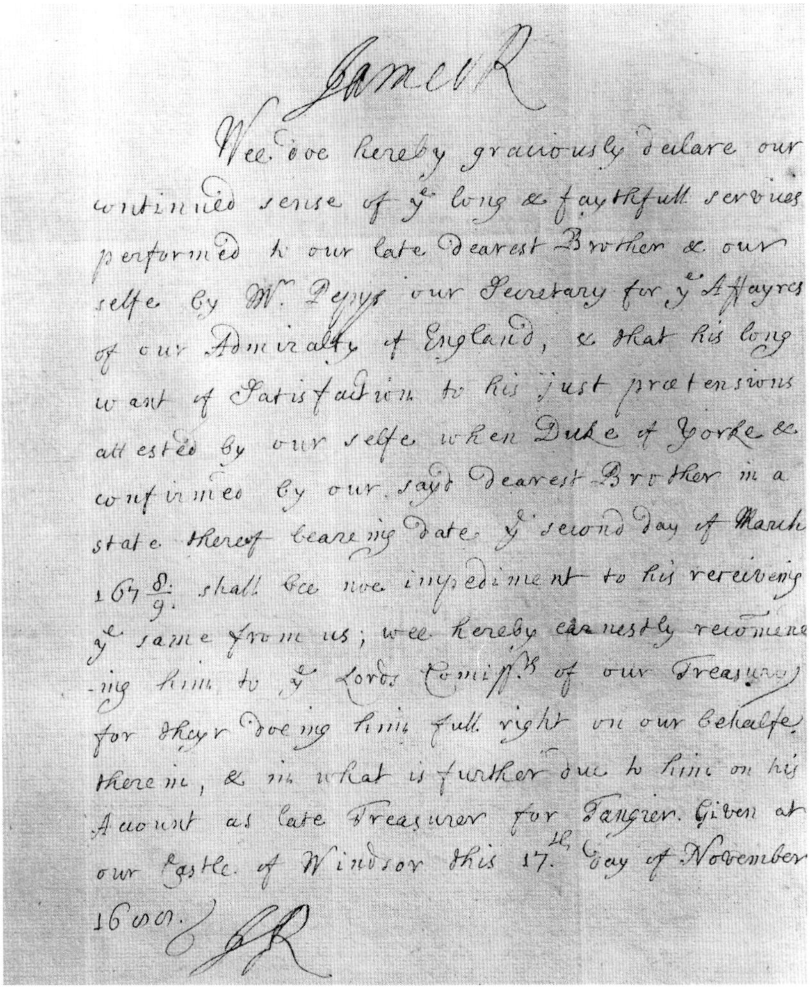

A document written by Samuel Pepys and signed twice by James II at Windsor on 17 November 1688 acknowledging money due to him for services to the Admiralty. James had left London to meet the invasion of Ireland by William of Orange. The sum, £28,000, was never paid to Pepys.

James was fully aware that he could not ensure toleration indefinitely by the exercise of his prerogative. He therefore devoted much effort to trying to pack a Parliament which would be committed to repealing the penal laws and the two Test Acts so that liberty of conscience would continue to prevail even after his own death. How far he might have succeeded is hard to say, but in any case before a new general election could be held, William of Orange landed in south-west England on 5 November 1688 with a considerable army. It now emerged that so dissatisfied had public opinion become with the King's clumsy and arbitrary way of acting that neither his army nor his navy would fight for him. Vainly the King made concessions to Protestant

opinion and dismissed the subservient but panic-stricken Earl of Sunderland. Soon after William landed, leading officers deserted the army which was concentrated at Salisbury to prevent a Dutch advance on London, and the entire navy later went over to William. James, who had been so brave when young, lost his nerve completely. He would not take command of the army; he sent his wife and baby son abroad; and after pretending to negotiate with William for the summoning of a free Parliament, he fled from his capital. He was caught attempting to board a ship and bundled back to London, from where William allowed him to flee again. On Christmas Day he arrived in France.

James had shown himself to be impatient, arrogant and, as one contemporary remarked, 'a silly man'. He had little interest in the arts or sciences, was over-sexed and a poor judge of men. Conscious of his father's fate on the scaffold, he surrendered his throne too easily to his son-in-law. Even when he managed to raise a Catholic army in Ireland and had the benefit of French military advice, he lost the battle of the Boyne against William largely through his own incompetence (1 July 1690). He spent most of the rest of his life in some comfort at St Germain, piously regretting his sins. Some historians believe that he was mentally defective in his last years, but there is no firm evidence for that. He continued to hunt and philander until he died of a stroke at the age of sixty-six.

A contemporary engraving of James II's flight from Ireland into exile in 1690, after his defeat by William of Orange at the battle of the Boyne. The military prowess of James's youth deserted him when faced by his son-in-law in Ireland.

# WILLIAM III *r.* 1688-1702
# and MARY II *r.* 1688-94

THE MARRIAGE OF THE TWO FUTURE monarchs took place in St James's Palace in London on 4 November 1677, which was William's twenty-sixth birthday. They were married for reasons of state. When Mary, the elder daughter of the Roman Catholic Duke of York, was informed that she was to be wedded to a stranger and a foreigner she wept for two days. William, who was asthmatic and slightly hunchbacked as well as reserved and taciturn, was hardly an attractive prospect, although the English public was delighted that Mary was to be 'embraced in Protestant arms'. She was then a pretty girl of fifteen, brought up in the Church of England, and her love life had hitherto consisted of a highly imaginative and platonic affair with an older lady of the court. Though a strict Calvinist, William had sown his wild oats, but since the age of twenty had been too deeply engaged in politics and war in the United Netherlands to have much time for frivolity. He had received an excellent education, was a master of languages and a connoisseur, as Mary was to be. The marriage worked out as well as most.

William, a posthumous son, had been brought up first by a formidable grandmother and later as a 'child of the state'. He was the great-grandson of William the Silent who helped form the independent Dutch Republic. But his father, Prince William II of Orange, who was ambitious, had quarrelled with the powerful Regents who constituted the wealthy governing class of Holland, and they strongly reacted against the House of Orange. The Regents and their leader, John de Witt, the Grand Pensionary of Holland, were determined to prevent the boy Prince from being appointed to his father's posts of Captain-General of the United Netherlands and Statholder or chief executive

*Opposite*: Portrait of Queen Mary II from the studio of Sir Godfrey Kneller. Mary was fifteen when she married the Calvinist William.

THE PORTRAICTVRE OF THE MOST ILLVSTRIOVS &
Noble, William of Nassau Prince of Orange, *&c* borne 1627
& maried 23 May, 1641.
*Are to be sold, by Tho: Ienner at the old Exhange,*

William of Orange, who upon his arrival in England told the crowd: 'I come to do you goot; I am here for all your goots.'

of Holland. De Witt allied himself with the French monarchy in 1662, but when five years later the King of France, Louis XIV, launched an aggressive war upon the Spanish Netherlands (modern Belgium), which lay between France and the United Netherlands, thus endangering Dutch security, the Grand Pensionary formed a triple alliance

with England and Sweden to restrain French territorial demands. Although it is doubtful whether
Louis XIV concluded peace with Spain because of
the formation of this triple alliance, he was angry
that the upstart Dutch republicans, whom he had
earlier befriended, should defy him. Louis succeeded in detaching King Charles II of England,
William's uncle, and the Swedish government
from the Dutch alliance and with the connivance
of Charles and the assistance of the English navy
directed an unprovoked attack on the Dutch in
1672. Thus threatened the Dutch overthrew de
Witt as a Francophile and called up on the
twenty-year-old William III, Prince of Orange
and Count of Nassau, to lead them against the
French as their Captain-General and Admiral-
General. For six years the young Prince resisted
French aggression by every political and military
means at his disposal. When peace was eventually

*Above*: Miniature depicting
William and Mary.

*Following pages:*
Contemporary oil painting
of William, showing his
customary flair for fighting,
at the battle of the Boyne,
which ended James II's reign.

The coronation of William
and Mary. Although his reign
officially began in 1689,
William had been exercising
administrative authority since
the Christmas of 1688.

concluded in 1678 the Dutch did not have to make any concessions whatsoever. William became not only the hero of his countrymen but also a Protestant champion in Europe.

William never forgave the French for this blatant attempt to subdue his small country. His uncle, Charles II, who withdrew in a humiliated way from the war in 1674, was anxious to gain prestige as an intermediary between the French and the Dutch. At first he aimed to please his nephew by carving a little kingdom for him out of the dismembered republic, but William was not to be bribed. Then Charles wanted William to use his influence with the Dutch States-General to accept a mediated peace. William refused to discuss the latter proposal until he had concluded his dynastic marriage with Princess Mary, which would draw together, at least symbolically, the English and Dutch peoples in resisting French ambitions. There is no doubt that this marriage impressed and annoyed Louis XIV. A mediated peace came next year. As the elder daughter of James, Duke of York, Mary was after her father the heir presumptive to the English and Scottish thrones. William soon found himself in an extremely awkward situation because his father-in-law was an avowed Roman Catholic and the great majority of the English House of Commons (from which Roman Catholics were excluded by a Test Act of 1678) were determined that James should be stopped from succeeding. It was even believed that the Popish Plot had been concocted to murder Charles II and to replace him by his Catholic brother. There was no such plot; but the Whigs or Exclusionists were committed to preventing James from coming to the throne and to replacing him either by his daughter Mary, William's wife, or by the Duke of Monmouth.

In 1681 William again visited England, Charles II hoping that he would assuage the anxieties of the Exclusionists. William was naturally cautious. He did not want to jeopardise his wife's hereditary rights, but on the other hand he did not wish the English monarchy to be so weakened by internal squabbles that it became a dependant of France. Charles for his part would not accept exclusion at any price and he did in fact count as a last resort on French protection to shield him from rebellion at home. In the end he skilfully defeated the Exclusionist movement, thus enabling William's father-in-law to succeed peacefully to the throne.

William viewed the whole political situation in England not so much from the point of view of religious controversy or personal ambition as in the context of Europe as a whole. By the 1680s the

French had overrun much of Western Europe and therefore, above all, William wanted to preserve a close friendship with England as a counterweight to Louis XIV's undimmed aims for glorious expansion. Although an Anglo-Dutch treaty was renewed in 1685, the danger was that his father-in-law would alienate his subjects by granting too many concessions to his fellow religionists and thus provoke a rebellion which would paralyse English influence on the continental mainland. His relations with James II were thus ambivalent. James was willing to be friendly only if both William and Mary would give their open support to the repeal of the anti-Catholic Penal and Test Acts. Both

The departure of William of Orange from Briel in 1688. William intervened in the affairs of England to prevent a predominance of Catholic ministers in the court of James II pushing the state into closer relations with Louis IX of France.

refused to do so since they were afraid that the predominance of Roman Catholic ministers and advisers in England would carry the kingdom over into the French camp even if this did not cause an insurrection. That was why ultimately William felt compelled to intervene actively in England in 1688 at the time when Louis XIV was launching large armies into Germany.

The Revolution of 1688, as it was called, though actually it was a Dutch invasion welcomed by English Protestants, was a bloodless success. To William's relief, since his father-in-law had left the kingdom it could be argued that he had 'abdicated' or 'deserted' his throne. It was not until early February in 1689 that a 'convention' or Parliament met which invited William and Mary to become King and Queen with the executive authority in William's hands. Thus it could be asserted that their reign did not begin until 1689; but in fact William had exercised administrative authority since Christmas 1688. Before they were offered the Crown William and Mary were asked to agree to a Declaration of Rights (subsequently converted into a Bill) which condemned the way in which James II had used his prerogative, particularly by dispensing with the laws. They agreed to this in general terms so that in effect a limited monarchy was established. Mary, who came to England in mid-February and put a cheerful face on things (for which she was censured by some as having usurped the throne of her father), had made it clear from the beginning that she had no intention of seeking a superior or even an equal position to her husband. She was content to love and obey him, but was willing to preside over the government during his absences abroad.

In fact substantial constitutional changes took place in the course of William's reign. An Act of Indulgence permitted Christian nonconformists (but not Roman Catholics) to worship freely subject to specific conditions; a Triennial Act required a new Parliament to be summoned every three years; a Mutiny Act prevented the employment of a standing army in times of peace without the consent of the Commons; a Civil List Act gave the Commons control over the King's expenditure, and indeed when he attempted to appropriate money from forfeitures of land in Ireland there was a rumpus. Finally in 1701 an Act of Settlement was passed which, among other things, not only provided for the Protestant succession, but required future monarchs specifically to be members of the Church of England, and forbade them to leave the kingdom without Parliamentary permission. Judges

LONDRES

were not to be dismissed without the approval of Parliament. (William did not in fact try to do so.) Other clauses, which would have hampered the evolution of Cabinet government, did not become effective. But possibly the most important event to take place in the reign of William and Mary was the establishment of the Bank of England, which, by enabling the government to borrow money in a sensible way, was to simplify foreign and colonial problems.

William's main concern was the war which broke out in Europe even before he had become King. Though the Holy Roman Emperor and the Dutch Republic had agreed to ally themselves in May 1680 so as to prevent the French mastery of Europe, it was not until September that William was able to induce the English people to accede to what became known as the first Grand Alliance. Then he had to campaign in

French hand-coloured woodcut *c.* 1700 entitled 'London, Capital City of the Kingdom of England'. In 1694 the Bank of England was established in London to provide for secure long-term government borrowing and the credit necessary for the expansion of trade and financing of overseas policies.

Ireland before himself engaging upon fighting the French in Flanders. He proved himself a fairly capable general, his chief success being the capture in September 1694 of the heavily fortified town of Namur against a French covering army. The peace of Ryswick, concluded in 1697, reduced French power. Afterwards William devoted his efforts to averting another major European war by negotiating two treaties defining the partition of the Spanish Empire when its childless ruler died. Unfortunately neither of them worked and the English Parliament blamed him for his secret diplomacy.

Queen Mary, whose influence had considerable effect on the moral climate of the court and country, died of smallpox in December 1694 at the age of thirty-three. William wrote to a friend just before her death: 'You can imagine what a state I am in, loving her as I do. You know what it is to have a good wife.' Though he was pressed to do so, he did not marry again. William was never a congenial king and indeed his popularity diminished after his wife's death and as memories of the causes of the revolution of 1688 faded. His original attempt to govern by employing more or less non-party men as his ministers did not really succeed, although he had a gift for discovering capable (but not always loyal) administrators. His difficulty was that whereas he could not be called a 'Tory king', he disliked the Whigs because their aim was to limit monarchical authority. Furthermore the Tories were 'Little Englanders' while the Whigs were more anti-French, which better suited his taste. He was able, however, to provide for the succession by reconciling himself with Princess Anne, Mary's younger sister, who had quarrelled with her, and by appointing Anne's friend, John Churchill, Earl of Marlborough, to be commander-in-chief and the architect of a second Grand Alliance against France when the danger of another war over the partition of the Spanish Empire loomed up. Before William died on 8 March 1702 his only regret was that he could not live to witness the final defeat of Louis XIV's France.

*Opposite*: Mary II lying in state. She died from smallpox in December 1694 at the age of thirty-three. William's popularity faded after her death and, despite being pressed, he never remarried.

# ANNE *r.* 1702-14

T HE SECOND DAUGHTER OF THE future James II by his first wife, Anne Hyde, was born on 6 February 1665. As her likelihood of succeeding to the throne appeared to be remote she was uneducated and untrained for the profession of monarchy, while her husband, Prince George of Denmark, whom she married in 1683 and loved dearly, was an amiable nonentity, who preferred being in the background. On the whole, Anne led an unhappy life. Though she had seventeen children, not one of them survived for long; her son William, Duke of Gloucester, was hydrocephalic and lived for only eleven years.

When Anne became Queen she was in permanent pain. Modern doctors are not in agreement about her precise maladies, but contemporaries called it gout. Being stout and unwieldy she often had to be moved on chairs or by pulleys. Her chief amusements were playing cards, drinking tea and admiring gardens; but she disliked fresh air. Her passionate affection for Sarah Churchill, the future Duchess of Marlborough, which began before she was married, was to give her much pleasure and later much pain. Sarah's voluminous writings have been largely relied upon by Anne's biographers as a basis for assessing her character, but it has to be remembered that what Sarah recorded was chiefly written after they had quarrelled. The fact was that Anne was an extremely conscientious Queen – though she had her personal prejudices – and was also a stout pillar of the Church of England. The bounty which she established out of her private resources for the benefit of the poorer clergy kept her name respected among churchmen long after she was dead.

When William III invaded England in 1688 it had evidently been arranged between Anne's friends, Bishop Compton and John and Sarah

*Opposite*: A portrait of Queen Anne by Edmund Lilly, painted a year after she succeeded to the throne. Although untrained for the role of monarch she was a diligent and hard-working queen. She is wearing the necklace of the order of the Garter, with its emblem of the dragon-slaying St George.

Lady Fitzharding.

Sarah Dutchess of Marlborough, Wife to John 1st Duke of Marlborough.

Churchill, that they would all desert her father in favour of her sister Mary's husband. For both Mary and Anne were devout Protestants and genuinely believed that James II had been using autocratic methods to catholicise England. The two sisters were also convinced that the son born to James by his second wife in June 1688 was suppositious. The letters that they wrote to each other sustaining this view are rather revolting. In any case it was a blow to James when both his daughters deserted him. After he went into exile Anne acquiesced in the decision made by Parliament that William should rule England during his lifetime, thus postponing her own right to succeed to the throne until after his death on the assumption, which proved correct, that William and Mary had no children. She rejoiced in an income of £50,000 a year voted her by Parliament and she moved into her own palace known as the Cockpit, on the site of the present Downing Street.

Unfortunately she was to be on bad terms for nearly five years with her sister, Queen Mary. The reason for this was that John Churchill, who had been created Earl of Marlborough by William and who had served him brilliantly during the Irish campaign, did not consider that he had been adequately rewarded for his services at the Revolution and therefore engaged in political intrigue against the King while Sarah remained Anne's closest friend. How far it was Churchill's intention to make use of the Jacobites (the followers of James II) in these intrigues is not clear. But Anne herself was conscious of guilty feelings over the way in which she had treated her father and even appears to have written him a contrite letter. William was fully aware of these intrigues in which not only Marlborough but some of his ministers engaged, but he was magnanimous enough to ignore them. For a short time Marlborough was deprived of his offices and put in the Tower of London. Mary naturally enough sided with her husband, thinking it was monstrous that Anne should keep Marlborough's wife so close to her. When Anne refused to dismiss Sarah from her service, she was obliged to leave Whitehall and sever relations with the King and Queen. It was not until after Mary's death that a reconciliation was effected with her brother-in-law. Then William restored Anne and John Churchill to his favour. Meanwhile Sarah had given birth to four healthy daughters which made her feel very superior to Anne, whom she treated with some condescension. Her eldest daughter, Henrietta, was married to Francis, only child of Sidney Godolphin, one of King William's ablest ministers. Thus Anne, the Churchills and Godolphin

*Opposite*: Sir Godfrey Kneller's painting of Sarah Marlborough playing cards with Lady Fitzharding. Anne had a deep affection for Sarah, although she was later to alienate her when Sarah's attitude became condescending and she took to staying away from court.

became a closely-knit group. When after William's death in March 1702 Anne became Queen, she wrote to Sarah, whom she appointed her Mistress of the Robes: 'We four must never part until death mows us down with his impartial hand.'

Anne, like William, tried at first to govern with a Cabinet of non-party or all-party ministers. Marlborough, who took command of the English and Dutch armies when war with France began in May 1702, and Godolphin, whom at his suggestion Anne appointed Lord Treasurer, were really non-party men, though they were often described as Tories. But Anne tended to favour the Tories, first because they were enthusiastic supporters of the established Church and second because they upheld the royal prerogatives. For most of the reign England was involved in the war of the Grand Alliance against France, in which Marlborough won three notable victories as well as planning successful campaigns. The extreme Tories, however, were critical of Marlborough because they favoured naval warfare rather than the expensive commitment of the kingdom to continental campaigns on land.

Anne was upset by this and showed it. For she at once raised Marlborough to a dukedom, asked that he should be voted a generous income in perpetuity and poured offices and money into Sarah Marlborough's lap. After his great victory at Blenheim in 1704 she presented him with one of the royal estates at Woodstock in Oxfordshire and in the following year dismissed his chief Tory critic, her uncle the Earl of Rochester, while another Tory leader, the Earl of Nottingham, resigned from his post of Secretary of State and was replaced by Robert Harley who was also Speaker of the Commons. Godolphin, Marlborough and Harley became known as 'the Triumvirate' which concentrated on winning the war. After the general election of 1705 the Queen dismissed three more leading Tories and under pressure from Sarah Marlborough appointed another of her sons-in-law, the third Earl of Sunderland, to the important ambassadorship in Vienna.

Anne, though she had her own principles – for example she was a patriot and spoke of 'her English heart' – was strongly influenced by personal likes and dislikes. She could not abide Sunderland, an extreme Whig; she took to Harley, a moderate Tory. Thus she resented it when after Whig compulsion in the House of Commons she was obliged to accept Sunderland as one of her Secretaries of State. Marlborough, Sunderland's father-in-law, and Godolphin became increasingly sure that the war against France could only be won if the

*Opposite*: Sir Godfrey Kneller's 1688 painting of Queen Anne presenting the plans of Blenheim Palace to Military Merit. The Queen presented the royal estate at Woodstock, Oxfordshire, to the Duke of Marlborough after his victory at Blenheim in 1704.

The articles of the Union presented to Queen Anne in 1706, taken from the 1786 publication *Historic Acts of the Queens of England*.

support given it by the Whigs in Parliament was reinforced by the presence of all the leading Whigs in the government. Harley, on the other hand, who had proved himself an able statesman and contributed markedly to the formation of the union with Scotland, of which the Queen approved and which was celebrated in May 1707, professed still to believe in the virtues of a central coalition government. Gradually, partly through the help of Abigail Masham, one of the Queen's ladies-in-waiting, Harley came to exert so much influence over the Queen, visiting her up the backstairs, that Godolphin and Marlborough were perturbed. A keen rivalry between Harley and Godolphin eventually culminated in the dismissal of Harley, mainly because Anne was still dependent on Marlborough's military genius to win the war.

At a general election in May 1708 the Whigs won a majority in the Commons and the Queen was compelled to admit all the members of what was called 'the Whig junto' into her Cabinet. Thus in spite of another victory achieved by Marlborough at Oudenarde, 1708 was a sad year for Anne. In October her beloved husband died. She ceased to trust any members of her government, while her alienation from Sarah Marlborough, which had begun not long after her accession owing to Sarah's haughty attitude towards her as Queen, was increased by the fact that Sarah absented herself from her duties at court for long periods and devoted herself to pro-Whig propaganda.

But in 1709 the party tide turned. The kingdom was growing tired of the long and costly war, while Anne herself reflected these feelings. Also, she was half persuaded that her Church was 'in danger' especially since she was not allowed to appoint the bishops she herself preferred, who were usually High Churchmen. When in February 1710 a clergy-

The historic articles of Union between England and Scotland, agreed in 1707 and held in the House of Lords record office.

ENGLANDS GLORY.

man named Henry Sacheverell, who had delivered an outspoken attack on the Whig settlement after the Revolution of 1688, was impeached in Westminster Hall, Anne showed sufficient interest to follow the proceedings in person. Despite being condemned Sacheverell was punished extremely lightly, and a political reaction set in. Harley got in secret touch with the Queen, offering to relieve her from the thraldom of the extreme Whigs. Thereupon she plucked up sufficient courage to dismiss her faithful servant Godolphin almost as cavalierly as Charles II got rid of Clarendon or James II of Sunderland. Afterwards she was to regret having done so. Furthermore, as the French had gallantly resisted the threat of invasion in the previous year, heavy losses being inflicted upon Marlborough at the battle of Malplaquet, the war looked as if it were going on for ever.

Thus pro-Anglican emotions and anti-war sentiments were aired in the general election of 1710, which resulted in an overwhelming Tory

The battle of Malplaquet, 11 September 1709. The French fended off the threat of invasion by inflicting heavy casualties on the forces under the command of Marlborough. Malplaquet reinforced the conviction of many in England that there would be no end to the war.

*Opposite:* The Duke of Marlborough surveys his troops at the battle of Oudenarde in the Spanish Netherlands, 30 June 1708.

Dutch engraving depicting the signing of the Treaty of Utrecht on 11 April 1713. English military success in the War of the Spanish succession was confirmed at Utrecht, which established England as a force in Continental power politics.

victory. At the beginning of 1711 Anne dismissed Sarah from all her offices after some painful scenes, and at the end of the year Marlborough was also dismissed. Harley took office and another extremely able and highly ambitious Tory, Henry St John, Viscount Bolingbroke, assiduously if unscrupulously devoted himself to securing a separate peace with France. To make certain that both Houses of Parliament approved the peace, Anne agreed to create twelve additional Tory peers at one time. When she opened Parliament in 1713 she was able to give news of the

Treaty of Utrecht, which was by no means unfavourable to British interests; it was followed by another general election when once again the Tories won a victory.

But Harley's powers were failing fast and Anne dismissed him from office in July 1713. She distrusted Bolingbroke and preferred, even though her sufferings were culminating in a last and fatal illness, to hand the office of Lord Treasurer, virtually prime minister, to her old and trusted friend the Whiggish Earl of Shrewsbury; she also had a woman friend in the red-headed Duchess of Somerset, another moderate Whig. On 1 August 1714, still perplexed by the exigencies of party politics, the Queen died; her doctor said, 'I believe sleep was never more welcome to a weary traveller than death was to her.'

Anne's was a notable reign in British history because it saw not only the Union with Scotland but also the acquisition of territorial gains and economic privileges which led to the foundation of the first British Empire. What the Queen's personal contribution was is hard to measure but recently it has been contended that her reign was the first in which Parliamentary elections and party contests were genuinely significant. In her support first of a coalition government then of a moderate Whig government, then her reluctant acquiescence in a purely Whig government, and finally her approval of a peace-making Tory government, it is reasonable to argue that she exemplified the feelings of the majority of her subjects, doing her duty, sometimes reluctantly, sometimes harshly, as she understood it.

# INDEX

Page references in *italics* indicate illustrations and their captions, while those in **bold** indicate main references to monarchs.

# PICTURE CREDITS

Weidenfeld & Nicolson Archive: endpapers and pages 2, 17, 19, 22, 24, 29, 44, 48, 49, 52, 56, 58 (bottom), 59, 63, 70, 72, 76, 81 (both), 88, 99
The Bridgeman Art Library, London: pages 8, 18, 20-21, 25, 27, 30-31, 35, 41, 50, 57, 60-61, 65, 66, 71, 87, 91, 92, 95, 96, 97, 98, 100
theartarchive: pages 23, 28, 40, 45, 58 (top), 62, 69
Sotheby's Picture Library: pages 26, 32, 36, 74, 79, 85

Barnaby's Picture Library: pages 37, 80
Christie's Images: pages 38-39, 51, 55, 73
AKG London: pages 42-43
Popperfoto: page 46
Hulton Getty: pages 53, 77
Topham Picturepoint: pages 82-83